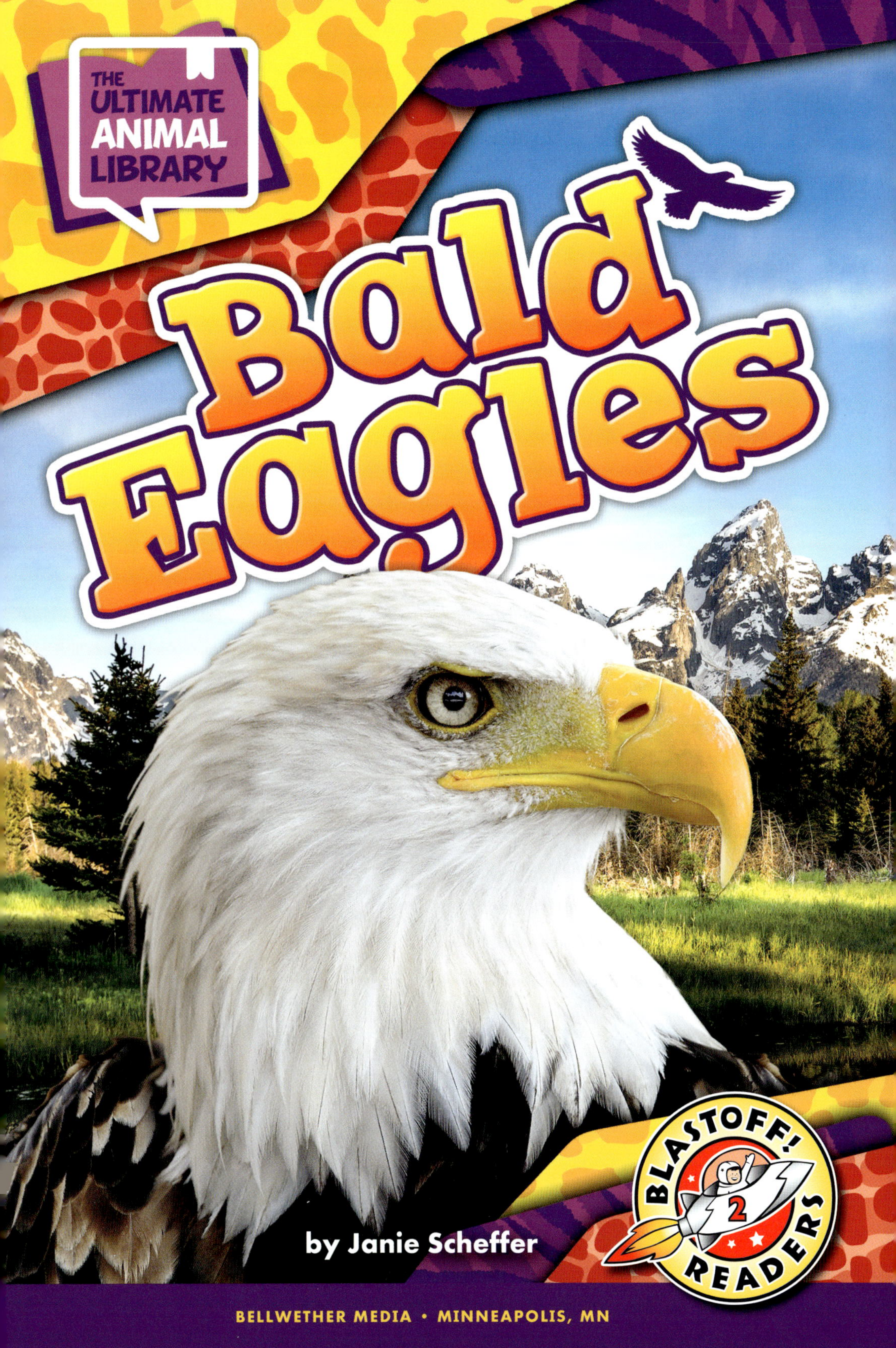
THE ULTIMATE ANIMAL LIBRARY
Bald Eagles
by Janie Scheffer
BLASTOFF! 2 READERS
BELLWETHER MEDIA • MINNEAPOLIS, MN

Blastoff! Readers are carefully developed by literacy experts to build reading stamina and move students toward fluency by combining standards-based content with developmentally appropriate text.

Level 1 provides the most support through repetition of high-frequency words, light text, predictable sentence patterns, and strong visual support.

Level 2 offers early readers a bit more challenge through varied sentences, increased text load, and text-supportive special features.

Level 3 advances early-fluent readers toward fluency through increased text load, less reliance on photos, advancing concepts, longer sentences, and more complex special features.

★ **Blastoff! Universe**

Reading Level

Grade K

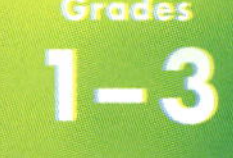

Grades 1–3

Grade 4

This edition first published in 2025 by Bellwether Media, Inc.

Library of Congress Cataloging-in-Publication Data

LC record for Bald Eagles available at: https://lccn.loc.gov/2024012093

Editor: Elizabeth Neuenfeldt   Series Designer: Veah Demmin

Printed in the United States of America, North Mankato, MN.

Table of Contents

What Are Bald Eagles?

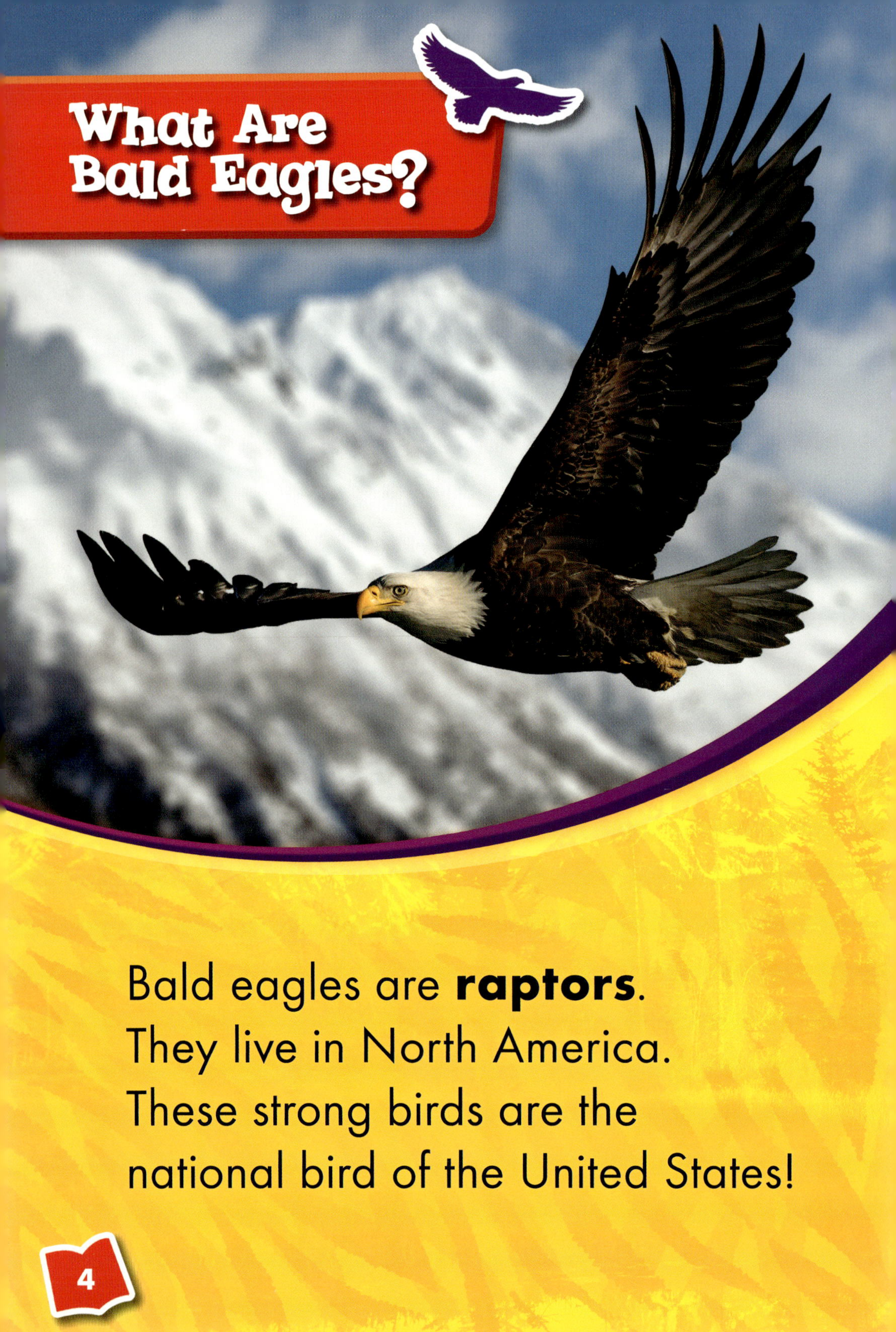

Bald eagles are **raptors**. They live in North America. These strong birds are the national bird of the United States!

Bald Eagle Report

Range

Habitats

forests

grasslands

wetlands

Bald eagles are big birds. They can weigh up to 14 pounds (6.4 kilograms).

Their **wingspans** can be up to 8 feet (2.4 meters) wide!

Adult bald eagles have white heads and tails. Their bodies are brown.

Their eyes, beaks, and feet are yellow.

Bald eagles have sharp beaks. They use their beaks to tear food apart.

Sharp **talons** on their feet help them catch their **prey**.

Spot a Bald Eagle

Big Nest Builders!

Bald eagles live in forests, **grasslands**, and **wetlands**. They fly between **perching sites**.

They make nests in trees. Their nests are often 6 feet (1.8 meters) wide!

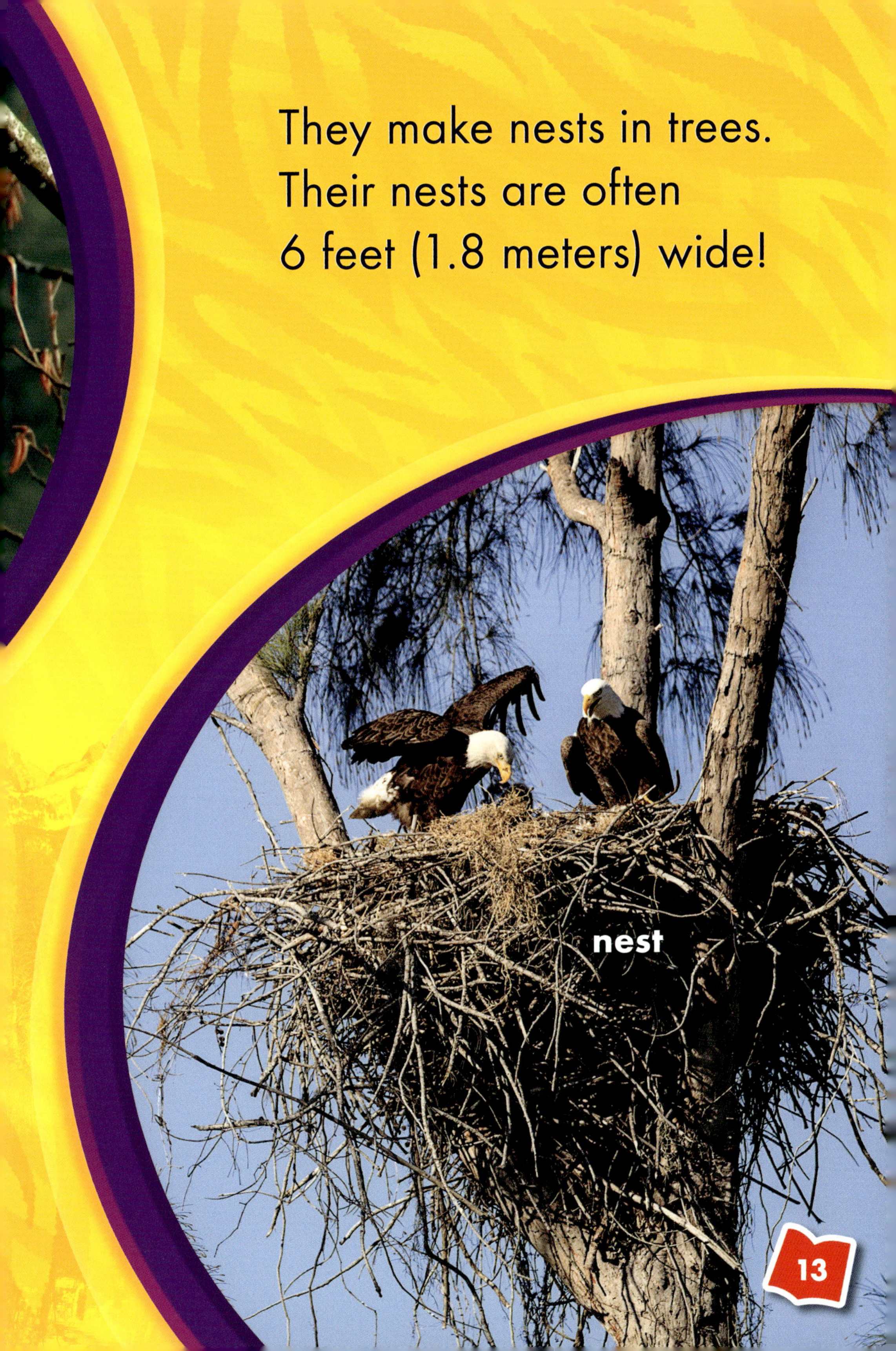

Bald eagles are great hunters. They can see prey from far away.

They mostly hunt fish. They also eat rabbits, birds, and **carrion**.

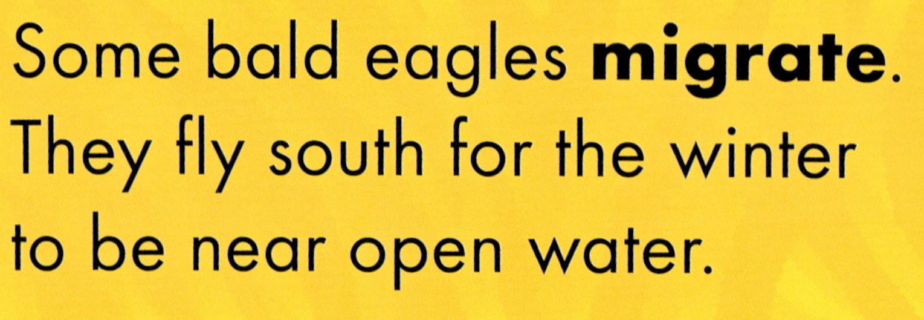

Some bald eagles **migrate**. They fly south for the winter to be near open water.

They may **roost** together in large groups.

Growing Up

Bald eagle pairs stay together for life.

Females lay one to three eggs each year. Eggs **hatch** in about 35 days. **Eaglets** are covered with gray **down**.

pair

down
eaglet

young eagle

Eagle pairs raise eaglets together. Eaglets fly when they are three months old.

Soon after, they leave the nest. At five years old, the young eagles become adults!

Glossary

carrion—the rotting meat of a dead animal

down—small, soft feathers that cover an eaglet's body

eaglets—baby eagles

grasslands—lands covered with grasses and other soft plants with few bushes or trees

hatch—to break open

migrate—to travel from one place to another, often with the seasons

perching sites—high-up resting or hunting spots

prey—animals hunted by other animals for food

raptors—large birds that hunt other animals; raptors have excellent eyesight and powerful talons.

roost—to rest in high places

talons—sharp claws on birds that allow them to grab and tear into their food

wetlands—areas of land that are covered with low levels of water for most of the year

wingspans—measurements of the distance from the tip of one wing to the tip of the other wing

To Learn More

AT THE LIBRARY

Earley, Christina. *Bald Eagle.* New York, N.Y.: Crabtree Publishing Company, 2023.

Kenney, Karen Latchana. *Lakes.* Minneapolis, Minn.: Bellwether Media, 2022.

Taylor, Charlotte. *Bald Eagles: Raptors on the Hunt.* New York, N.Y.: Enslow Publishing, 2022.

ON THE WEB

FACTSURFER

Factsurfer.com gives you a safe, fun way to find more information.

1. Go to www.factsurfer.com.
2. Enter "bald eagles" into the search box and click 🔍.
3. Select your book cover to see a list of related content.

Index

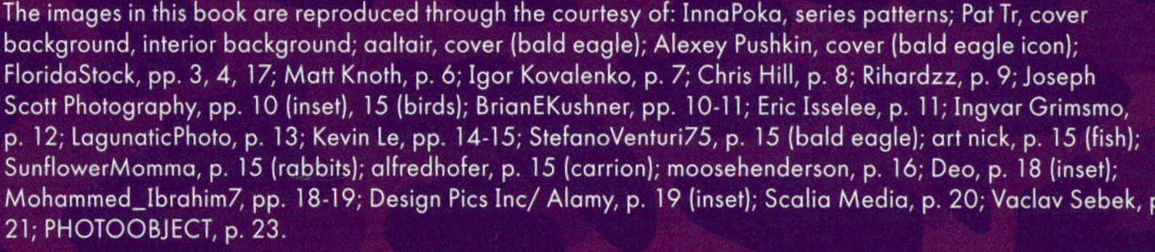

The images in this book are reproduced through the courtesy of: InnaPoka, series patterns; Pat Tr, cover background, interior background; aaltair, cover (bald eagle); Alexey Pushkin, cover (bald eagle icon); FloridaStock, pp. 3, 4, 17; Matt Knoth, p. 6; Igor Kovalenko, p. 7; Chris Hill, p. 8; Rihardzz, p. 9; Joseph Scott Photography, pp. 10 (inset), 15 (birds); BrianEKushner, pp. 10-11; Eric Isselee, p. 11; Ingvar Grimsmo, p. 12; LagunaticPhoto, p. 13; Kevin Le, pp. 14-15; StefanoVenturi75, p. 15 (bald eagle); art nick, p. 15 (fish); SunflowerMomma, p. 15 (rabbits); alfredhofer, p. 15 (carrion); moosehenderson, p. 16; Deo, p. 18 (inset); Mohammed_Ibrahim7, pp. 18-19; Design Pics Inc/ Alamy, p. 19 (inset); Scalia Media, p. 20; Vaclav Sebek, p. 21; PHOTOOBJECT, p. 23.